Saint Francis

and the Problem of Possessions

Other volumes for this series:

Saint Francis
and the Problem of Possessions

Primary Sources from
Francis of Assisi: Early Documents
for Devotional Use

Jon M. Sweeney
series editor

Francis of Assisi Spiritual Practices series

NEW CITY PRESS
Enkindling the Spirit of Unity

Published by New City Press
202 Comforter Blvd.,
Hyde Park, NY 12538
www.newcitypress.com

Library of Congress Control Number: 2023930675

ISBN: 978-1-56548-556-3 (paper)
ISBN: 978-1-56548-559-4 (e-book)

Printed in the United States of America

Contents

General Introduction

The *Francis of Assisi Spiritual Practices* series utilizes the texts and translations of New City's groundbreaking and now complete *Francis of Assisi: Early Documents, Volumes 1-4* (1999-2020) to offer readers of all backgrounds inspiring, encouraging, and challenging entry-points to the essential issues of a Christian life in the twenty-first century. Each book in the series should appeal particularly to readers who desire to walk the Way of Saint Francis with relevance to his life, writings, and legacy. We created the series with the conviction that the Way of Francis is as relevant today as it was eight hundred years ago.

The first four volumes have been planned. The one you are holding, *Saint Francis and the Problem of Possessions*, is the second. These are the other three:

- *Saint Francis and the Way of Lent* (already available)
- *Saint Francis and How We Relate to Fellow Creatures* and
- *Saint Francis and the Big, Wide, Lay-led Church*

Each book stands on its own, presenting one important aspect of the spirituality of the world's most popular saint.

A four-week format is designed for both individual and group use. Each week, or chapter, focuses the reader on a theme that is central to that volume's overall theme. Short introductions are written by the editor and designed to preface selections from the primary texts from the *Francis of Assisi: Early Documents* volumes, and these are each followed by questions for discussion or reflection. There are six readings for each week, followed by final prayers of intention and spiritual practice suggestions for that week on that theme.

We would love to hear from you, as to how you are using these books, and how to improve them for future editions. Also, our hope is to continue this series with additional titles, as demand and time and God permits. Your feedback will be an important step along the way for us to do that well. Please write to us at newseries@ newcitypress.com. *Pace e bene.*

Jon M. Sweeney
Series Editor

Introduction to this Volume

One of the first things people seem to know about Saint Francis is that he lived in solidarity with the poor. He grew up in a wealthy home—his father was a merchant of fancy silks—but he gave this up in young adulthood to identify with Jesus, who Francis believed with all his heart was literally and intentionally poor. Francis was then a follower of the God who became a human being in the person of a poor man and lived a poor life, among poor people, despite the fact that many of those people expected him, as their savior, to be powerful, royal, and even wealthy.

The list of saints who have been inspired by Francis's particular poverty is also noteworthy. It is a long and important list that includes, even in the twentieth century, Charles de Foucauld, Dorothy Day, and Mother Teresa.

Living among the "poorest of the poor" in the slums of Calcutta, Mother Teresa took a vow of poverty that resembled closely Francis's life and teachings, and deliberately so. Referring to his example, she often insisted that she and her fellow Missionaries of Charity eat as the poor of Calcutta eat and wear clothing that is like what they wear. She would quote Francis in this regard, referring to his teaching to own few clothes and to patch them frequently.[1]

---

1. See *Teresa of Calcutta: Active Love, Dark Night,* by Jon M. Sweeney (Collegeville, MN: Liturgical Press, 2022), see chapter 3.

But these teachings did not originate with Francis. He always believed that what he was doing was simply an imitation of what Jesus did and taught his followers to do. So, what did Jesus say about poverty that gave Francis such passion for living this way?

To his disciples, most of whom were already poor, Jesus said in the Sermon on the Mount:

> Blessed are you who are poor, for yours is the kingdom of God.
> Blessed are you who are hungry now, for you will be filled.
> Blessed are you who weep now, for you will laugh. (Lk 6:20-21)

And, before they could even join Jesus as his disciples, he told them:

> If you wish to be perfect, go, sell your possessions, and give the money to the poor, and you will have treasure in heaven; then come, follow me. (Mt 19:21)

That was the starting point for following the will of God. Which is why the title of this study in the spirituality of Francis of Assisi makes sense only if we agree that possessions, in and of themselves, are often a hindrance to following Christ and living a Christian life.

Still, the matter is not so simple, and the chapter titles of this book—as they are, divided into "Weeks" in the manner of a devotional that one might use over the span of a month or so—are intended to reflect this complexity. There is the matter of stuff. Then there is the issue of money, meaning coins and bills in Francis's day, as well as credit and assets in our own time. These very practical approaches are then concluded with the more general principles found in Weeks Three and Four as we look at "Reimagining a Vow of Poverty" in our lives today, and the meaning of "Living Poor for Others"— because, after all, our spirituality is not for ourselves, but for others.

In his message to would-be Franciscans living otherwise secular lives, Pope Leo XIII in 1888 said, "The Third Order was born fitted to a multitude and thus it proclaims the monuments and reality of the just, integral, and religious morals of a superior age, as much as this is possible."[2] That is what we set out to investigate in this book of texts from the life and teachings of Saint Francis: how much is this possible?

2.   Pope Leo XIII, *Misericors Dei Filius*, "Constitution On the Law of the Franciscan Third Order Secular," May 30, 1888.

Week One

The Problem with Stuff

Many obstacles stand in the way of people who desire to live by Jesus's teaching, not the least of which is that we are separated from the milieu of those who heard Jesus preach in first century Palestine. Those listening to Jesus were Jews, and Jews were a sometimes protected, sometimes persecuted minority in an outlying district of the vast Roman Empire. The people lived largely separate from Roman life, in Jewish villages, attending Jewish schools, in communities ruled by laws interpreted by Jewish magistrates.[3]

But maybe we make too much of these differences. Two thousand years ago, in Palestine, there were those who had much, and those who had much less. So when Jesus began to talk about being poor, and the blessedness of the poor, his teaching was countercultural in a way that was true then, remains so today, and will remain so until the kingdom of God comes in its fullness.

Jesus taught that in poverty we know God, identify with God in Christ, and do our duty as people of faith. First, what about all our material possessions—our

---

3.   E. P. Sanders, *The Historical Figure of Jesus* (New York: Penguin Books, 1995), 20-21.

"stuff"? What should we do with it? Does it somehow stand in the way of knowing and following God in this way? It certainly stands in the way of modeling our lives after the Way of Saint Francis.

Francis famously gave all his stuff away, and instructed anyone who wanted to follow him in his way of life to do similarly. In the most memorable scenes, rarely shown in the movies or told in the books about Francis, the first friars disposed of their stuff as Francis waited nearby to be sure that they've done it.

Is that what we are supposed to do, still, today? When Jesus told the young man the first step to discovering the will of God—"If you wish to be perfect, go, sell your possessions, and give the money to the poor, and you will have treasure in heaven; then come, follow me" (Mt 19:21)—he did so with the disciples in earshot. The following verse is one of the saddest in the Gospels: "When the young man heard this word, he went away grieving, for he had many possessions" (Mt 19:22).

Jesus then turned to the disciples. The account goes like this:

> Then Jesus said to his disciples, "Truly I tell you, it will be hard for a rich person to enter the kingdom of heaven. Again I tell you, it is easier for a camel to go through the eye of a needle than for someone who is rich to enter the kingdom of God." When the disciples heard this, they were greatly astounded and said, "Then who can be saved?" But Jesus looked at them

and said, "For mortals it is impossible, but for God all things are possible." (Mt 19:23-26)

So, again, where does this leave us?

A student of early Franciscan history and theology knows that in the century after Francis's death this issue—the ownership of property, stuff—became a divisive point, pitting friars against each other. This even led to Pope John XXII to oppose Francis's teaching on poverty and rule, supposedly conclusively, in a papal bull of 1323, that stated it was heretical to say that Christ and the apostles owned nothing, carried no money, and other teachings that Francis had earlier made explicit.[4]

So ordinary pilgrims of the twenty-first century, as well as Franciscans from way back, have difficulty figuring out how to live by these Gospel principles!

---

4.   See David Burr, *The Spiritual Franciscans: From Protest to Persecution in the Century After Saint Francis* (University Park, PA: Pennsylvania State University Press, 2001), 274-77.

Reading 1

Let's set the scene: He has stripped himself in front of the bishop of Assisi, his father, and the whole town. He has been set upon by bandits and rolled in the snow; he has rebuilt the church of San Damiano; he has begun to preach penance in Assisi; and he still is all alone with God. Then come others wanting to join him.

The first is Bernard, older than Francis, well-respected in town, with wealth. Bernard spies on Francis as Francis stays overnight in Bernard's house, and witnesses the younger man in genuine prayer, and then decides the next morning to become his first follower.

The Life of Saint Francis
Thomas of Celano

Chapter 10: His Preaching the Gospel and Announcing Peace and the Conversion of the First Six Brothers[5]

He then began to preach penance to all with a fervent spirit and joyful attitude. He inspired his listeners with words that were simple and a heart that was heroic. His word was like a blazing fire, reaching the deepest parts of the heart, and filling the souls of all with wonder. He seemed entirely different from what he had been, and looking up to heaven he refused to look down upon

---

5. *Early Documents: Vol. 1 (The Saint)*, 202-203.

earth. It is truly amazing that he first began to preach where he had learned to read as a little boy, and where at first he was reverently buried.

In all of his preaching, before he presented the word of God to the assembly, he prayed for peace saying, "May the Lord give you peace." He always proclaimed this to men and women, to those he met and to those who met him. Accordingly, many who hated peace along with salvation, with the Lord's help wholeheartedly embraced peace. They became themselves children of peace, now rivals for eternal salvation.

Among these there was a man from Assisi with a holy and simple character, who was the first to follow devoutly the man of God.

After him, brother Bernard, embracing the delegation of peace, eagerly ran after the holy man of God to gain the kingdom of heaven. He had often received the blessed father as a guest, had observed and tested his life and conduct. Refreshed by the fragrance of his holiness, he conceived fear and gave birth to the spirit of salvation. He used to see him praying all night long, sleeping rarely, praising God and the glorious Virgin, His mother. He was amazed and said, "This man truly is from God." So he hurried to sell all he had and distributed it to the poor, not to his relatives. Grasping the title of a more perfect way, he fulfilled the counsel of the holy gospel: "If you wish to be perfect, go and sell all you own, and give to the poor, and you will have treasure in heaven; then come, follow me." When he had done this, he joined the holy man, Francis, in the same life and habit, and was always with him, until the brothers increased in number and he, with the obedience of his devoted father, was sent to other regions.

Reflect or Discuss

1. What evidence does Bernard seem to require, before deciding to turn his life upside down by following Francis?

2. What's the first thing Bernard does, before presuming to join Francis? (The implication is that he had heard from Francis that this is what was asked of anyone who desired to follow Christ.)

3. Early in this reading, the narrator relates: "It is truly amazing that he first began to preach where he had learned to read as a little boy." Why is this amazing?

4. Go to a Bible and read this verse in its original context: "If you wish to be perfect, go and sell all you own, and give to the poor, and you will have treasure in heaven; then come, follow me" (Mt 19:21). Was Francis right to expect the same of himself, and his followers, 1,200 years later?

Reading 2

Let's take a step back now. Friar Julian of Speyer tells the story beautifully of what Francis had heard from God, and how Francis incorporated what he heard into his preaching of penance, before Bernard and others came to follow him. Note: There are no surviving sermons of Francis to indicate what he precisely said when he "preached penance," which he often spoke of doing.

The Life of Saint Francis
Julian of Speyer

Chapter 3: How, Undertaking Evangelical Perfection, He Changed His Habit a Second Time, Preached and Began to Have Brother Companions; And How He Foreknew His and Their Future, Sent Them Two-by-Two Throughout the World, and Arranged Their Coming Together Again[6]

Blessed Francis had completed his work on the three churches, as has been said, and he had, up until that time, worn the habit of a hermit, carrying a staff in his hand, with shoes on his feet and a leather belt around his waist.

Now one day at Mass, he heard those things which Christ in the gospel spoke to his disciples who were sent out to preach: that they should not possess gold nor silver,

---

6.   *Early Documents: Vol. 1 (The Saint)*, 379-80.

nor carry a wallet along the way or a purse, or a walking stick or bread, nor have shoes or two tunics. And later, from the priest, he understood these instructions more fully and was soon filled with indescribable joy. "This," he said, "is what I seek, this is what I desire with all my heart." And so, after committing to memory everything he had heard he joyfully applied himself to carrying out these commands and removed his extra clothing without delay. From this moment on he never used a walking stick, shoes, purse, or wallet. Accordingly, he made a very cheap and plain tunic, and throwing the belt away, tied the tunic with a cord.

Applying all the care of his heart, to fulfill the words of the new grace he had heard, he became, by divine inspiration, the proclaimer of evangelical perfection and began publicly to preach penance with simplicity. Moreover, his statements were neither hollow nor ridiculous, but filled with the power of the Holy Spirit. They penetrated the marrow of the heart and provoked stunned amazement in those who heard them. But, as he himself later testified, he also learned by the Lord's revelation a greeting of this sort, that he should say: "May the Lord give you peace." Thus, in all his preaching, he greeted the people at the beginning of his talk with the proclamation of peace. Filled with the spirit of the prophets, he proclaimed peace and preached salvation, as the prophet said. And it happened that by counsels about salvation, he brought to true peace many who had previously lived at odds with Christ and far from salvation.

As the truth of Blessed Francis's simple teaching and life became known to many, some men soon began to be moved to penance by his example, and leaving all things, joined him in habit and life.

Reflect or Discuss

1. Possessing not gold or silver, and not carrying a wallet or purse, are lines from the synoptic gospels. See Mt 10:9-10, Mk 6:8-9, and Lk 9:3, 10:4.

2. Julian's account tells us that "from the priest, [Francis] understood these instructions more fully." This perhaps means that the text was read to him in Latin, the language of all bibles at that time. If Francis was biblically illiterate, what does that suggest, also, about his poverty?

3. How did Francis respond when he absorbed these teachings? Julian's account says that Francis did a few things right away.

4. It certainly seems that Francis connected the penance of life without possessions with salvation itself. What do you think this meant for him?

5. What does this mean for us? Perhaps the meaning is contained in defining "salvation"?

Reading 3

This episode from the early Life of Francis—until recently called "The Anonymous of Perugia"— recently has been identified as John of Perugia's *The Beginning or Founding of the Order.* It describes a scene we know took place in the spring of 1208.

Bernard and Peter have already joined Francis in his work and way of life and now here comes the third to join him, Giles. As soon as Giles joins the group, Francis seems to sense that he will be able to understand, and personally share in, this radically countercultural approach to Christianity. So, together they head for the road on the way to the Marches of Ancona, a somewhat remote part of the Papal States (and later, Italy) that quickly became a favorite spot for Francis and a rich source of converts to the Franciscan way.

It is interesting to look in on the emotional atmosphere that surrounds the two men as they walk together.

The Beginning or Founding of the Order
John of Perugia

From *Chapter 3: The First Place Where They Stayed and Persecution by Their Relatives*[7]

---

7. *Early Documents: Vol. 2 (The Founder)*, 40-41.

Blessed Francis then took Brother Giles with himself to the Marches of Ancona, while the other two remained behind. As they were going along, they rejoiced not a little in the Lord. Francis, the man of God, reveled in a very loud voice, singing out in French, praising and blessing the Lord.

Indeed they were filled with great joy, as if they had just acquired an immense treasure. They were able to rejoice so much because they had forsaken so much, and considered as dung the things over which people usually grieve. They regarded as bitter what people of the world consider desirable, things that bring about much misery and grief.

Then blessed Francis told his companion, Brother Giles: "Our religion will be like a fisherman who casts his nets into the water, catching a great number of fish. Seeing the large number of fish, he puts the big ones in his baskets, leaving the small ones in the water." Giles was astonished at the prophecy that the saint uttered, for he knew how few the brothers were.

The man of God did not yet preach to the people. But while they were going through towns and villages, he would encourage men and women to fear and love the Creator of heaven and earth and to do penance for their sins. Brother Giles would respond: "What he says is very good. Believe him."

Those who heard them would say to each other: "Who are these men, and what are these words they're saying?"

Some of them used to say that they seemed to be fools or drunkards, while others would say: "The words coming out of their mouths are not those of fools." One of them said: "Either they are clinging to the Lord for the sake of the highest perfection, or they have gone mad, for their physical life seems reckless. They walk barefoot, wear cheap clothing, and eat very little." Yet there was no one who followed them at that time. Young women, seeing them at a distance, would run away fearing they would be taken in by foolishness. Even though hardly anyone followed them, people remained nevertheless in awe at the holy way of life with which they seemed to be marked for the Lord's sake.

After they had traveled around that province, the brothers returned to Saint Mary of the Portiuncula.

Reflect or Discuss

1. What has happened to Francis? Before this, he was known as a man of severe penance. Is he still?

2. How does one combine a life of penance with singing joyfully? Do the two make sense together?

3. Note: the text tells us that Francis was not yet preaching to people. So, before he ever preached, he brought together in his life these two aspects of following Christ.

4. Why might people have been afraid to "be taken in by [such] foolishness"?

Reading 4

Here, the narrative we read yesterday from John of Perugia, continues. This is what happens next, including a statement from the Bishop of Assisi to Francis, and Francis's notable response.

The Beginning or Founding of the Order
John of Perugia

From *Chapter 3: The First Place Where They Stayed and Persecution by Their Relatives*[8]

After a few days had elapsed, three other men from Assisi, Brother Sabbatino, Brother John and Brother Morico the Short, came to them, humbly begging Blessed Francis to admit them into his company. He received them kindly and eagerly.

However, when they went about the city begging alms, scarcely anyone was willing to give to them; instead they would tell them: "You got rid of your own possessions, and now you want to eat those of others." Thus, they suffered extreme want. Even their relatives and families would persecute them. Others from that city—great and small, men and women—would scorn and ridicule them as senseless and stupid, except for the

---

8.   *Early Documents: Vol. 2 (The Founder)*, 41.

city's bishop to whom the blessed Francis frequently went to seek counsel.

The reason their families and relatives used to persecute them, while others ridiculed them, was because at that time you could not find anyone who would abandon all his possessions and go begging from door to door.

One day when the blessed Francis had gone to that bishop, the bishop told him: "It seems to me that your life is very rough and hard, not having or possessing anything in this world." The saint of God answered: "Lord, if we had any possessions, we would need arms to protect them because they cause many disputes and lawsuits. And possessions usually impede the love of God and neighbor. Therefore we do not want to possess anything in this world."

And this answer pleased the bishop.

Reflect or Discuss

> 1. A literalist regarding religious law and commandments might argue that disciples of Christ (and then, Francis) follow Mt 19:21 ("If you wish to be perfect, go, sell your possessions, and give the money to the poor, and you will have treasure in heaven; then come, follow me.") simply because it is commanded. No other explanation necessary. Do you think Francis saw it that way?

> 2. "Their physical life seems reckless," people said. What do you think of that accusation?

3. What do you think of the bishop's statement to Francis? (It was really a question. We might read it as: "Are you making your life unnecessarily difficult, by not having or possessing anything at all?")

4. Francis's answer to the bishop's question is, for many followers of Francis, the best way of understanding how to relate to possessions. Rather than having none at all, we might possess only what we are unwilling to defend. What do you think of that as a rule?

Reading 5

Perhaps the most famous text in the early Franciscan tradition about poverty is this allegorical one. Here, Poverty is personified—female and sacred—and Francis is seen pursuing her as a lover would do. Lady Poverty is composed of the sacred feminine Wisdom of biblical literature, as well as the holy Catholic Church.

We do not know who wrote it—perhaps it was Caesar of Speyer. Its original composition surely dates to the thirteenth century; some have said as early as 1227, just after Francis's death, and others have argued that it was written two generations later in the years immediately following the death of St. Bonaventure, in 1274.[9]

Here are two short selections from this text, the first from its Prologue, composed in a narrator's descriptive voice, and the second diving directly into the allegory.

---

9.   See the editors' discussion in *Early Documents: Vol. 1 (The Saint)*, 14-15 and 523-24. For example: "Gregory IX may well have unknowingly prompted the composition of . . . *The Sacred Exchange between Saint Francis and Lady Poverty.* [In] his papal decree, *Quo elongati,* September 28, 1230. . . . arguing as Francis's friend and advisor, Gregory declared that Francis's *Testament,* to which many were appealing as the only true interpretation of the Rule, was not binding. . . . [T]he document challenged the foundations of the Order, especially its pursuit of poverty. *The Sacred Exchange* was not simply a response. It was an appeal to return to the lofty idealism of poverty upon which the primitive fraternity of Francis and his first brothers had been built" (15).

The Sacred Exchange between Saint Francis and Lady
Poverty[10]
Caesar of Speyer?

From the prologue

Among the other outstanding and exceptional virtues which prepare in us an abode and a dwelling for God and which show an excellent and unencumbered path of going to and arriving before Him, holy Poverty shines with a certain prerogative before them all. By a unique grace, it excels the claims of the others. For it is the foundation and guardian of all virtues and enjoys a principal place and name among the gospel virtues. As long as they have been firmly placed on this foundation, the others need not fear the downpour of rains, the rush of floods, and the blast of winds that threaten ruin.

This is certainly appropriate since the Son of God, the Lord of virtue and the King of glory, fell in love with this virtue with a special affection. He sought, found, and embraced it while achieving our salvation in the middle of the earth. At the beginning of his preaching he placed it as a light of faith in the hands of those entering the gate, and even set it as the foundation stone of the house. While the other virtues receive the kingdom of heaven only by way of promise from Him, poverty is invested with it by Him without delay. Blessed, he said, are the poor in spirit, for the kingdom of heaven is theirs.

---

10.   *Early Documents: Vol. 1 (The Saint)*, 529, 530.

From the section *Blessed Francis Asks about Poverty*

He eagerly began to go about the streets and piazzas of the city, as a curious explorer diligently looking for her whom his soul loved. He asked those standing about, inquired of those who came near him: "Have you seen her whom my soul loves?" But that saying was hidden from them as though it was barbaric. Not understanding him, they told him: "We do not know what you're saying. Speak to us in our own language and we will answer you."

At that time there was no voice and no sense among Adam's children of being willing to converse with or to speak to anyone about poverty. They hated it with a vengeance, as they do even today, and could not speak peacefully to anyone asking about it. Therefore, they answered him as they would a stranger and declared that they did not know anything of what he was seeking.

Reflect or Discuss

1. Right from the start, poverty is imagined as the setting or "abode" for God in us. What do you think that means? How does it relate to the birth of Christ—and to Francis's affection for the Nativity and creche?

2. How might poverty be the "guardian of all virtues," as this text claims it to be?

3. This allegory adds to what we know from the biographies of Francis. We see Francis going about Assisi inquiring after "her whom his soul loved." This is not a girl! She is Poverty. Does this alter your image of the saint?

4. How does the inability of most people to understand Francis's seeking this love relate to Jesus preaching parables in Mark 4:1-34? Jesus said, "Let anyone with ears to hear listen!" and then, to the disciples, "To you has been given the secret of the kingdom of God, but for those outside, everything comes in parables" (vv. 9, 11).

Reading 6

We conclude this Week's theme with one last selection from the great allegorical work, "The Sacred Exchange between Saint Francis and Lady Poverty," which was designed to explain Francis's love of poverty and the necessity for any would-be Franciscan to follow him in that passionate pursuit and embrace. The allegorical qualities of the story (personification of Poverty; polarization of opposites; both literal and figurative meanings) come through clearly here.

The figure of Lady Poverty is meant to closely resemble God in the feminine form of Wisdom, or Sophia in the Greek, personified at times in the Book of Proverbs, and most of all in the Book of Wisdom. These are both portions of the Hebrew scriptures, after the Torah. Remember that these are portions of scripture that refer to God in the feminine.

The Sacred Exchange between Saint Francis and Lady Poverty[11]
Caesar of Speyer?

After he left the city . . . blessed Francis quickly came to a certain field in which, as he looked from afar, he saw two old men wasted away from great sorrow. . . . Francis. . . said to them: "Tell me, I beg you, where does

---

11. *Early Documents: Vol. 1 (The Saint)*, 531-32.

Lady Poverty dwell? Where does she eat? Where does she rest at noon, for I languish with love of her?"

But they answered: "Good brother, we have sat here for a time and for times and for half a time. We have frequently seen her pass by for there are many searching for her. Sometimes many accompanied her, but she returned alone and naked, not adorned with any jewels, nor graced with any companions, nor wearing any clothes. She used to weep bitterly and say 'The children of my mother have fought against me.' And we said to her: 'Be patient, for the upright love you.'

"Brother, she has now gone up to a great and high mountain where God has placed her. She is dwelling in the sacred mountains because God loved her above all the tabernacles of Jacob. Giants have not been able to touch the footprints of her steps and eagles cannot fly even to her shoulder. Poverty is the only thing that everyone condemns so that it cannot be discovered in the land of those living comfortably. She is hidden from their eyes, then, and concealed from the birds of the sky. God understands her path and He knows her place.

"If, then, you wish to reach her, brother, take off your clothes of rejoicing, and put aside every burden and sin clinging to you for, unless you are naked, you will not be able to climb to her who lives in so high a place. Yet, because she is kind, she will easily be seen by those who love her and be found by those who search for her. To think about her, brother, is perfect understanding, and whoever keeps vigil for her will quickly be secure. Take faithful companions so that during the mountain's ascent you will have their advice and be strengthened by their help. For woe to the one who is alone! If he falls, he will have no one to lift him up. For if anyone falls, he should have someone help him!"

After receiving the advice of such men, then, blessed Francis came and chose some faithful companions for himself with whom he hurried to the mountain. He said to his brothers: "Come, let us climb the mountain of the Lord and the dwelling of Lady Poverty that she might teach us her ways and we might walk in her paths."

Because of its great height and difficulty, they studied the ascent of the mountain from every angle. Some of them said to one another: "Who can climb this mountain and who can reach its summit?"

Blessed Francis understood this and said to them: "The road is difficult, brothers, and the gate that leads to it is narrow. There are few who find it. Be strengthened in the Lord and in the power of his virtue for everything difficult will be easy for you. Cast off the burdens of your own will, get rid of the weight of your sins, and gird yourselves as powerful men. Forgetting whatever is in the past, stretch yourselves as much as you can for what lies ahead. I tell you that wherever you place your foot will be yours. For the Spirit is before your face, Christ the Lord, Who draws you to the heights of the mountain in bonds of love."

Reflect or Discuss

1. Dorothy Day, as a Catholic Worker, lived in voluntary poverty and wrote often on the subject. She once quoted a letter from a priest to the *Catholic Worker* newspaper in which he reminded her of keeping precarity as well as poverty. She quoted him thus: "Nowadays religious communities are good, I am sure, but they are mistaken about poverty. They accept, admit, poverty on principle, but everything must be good and strong, buildings must be fireproof. Precarity is everywhere rejected, and precarity is an essential element of poverty. This has been forgotten. Here in our monastery we want precarity in everything except the church. These last days our refectory was near collapsing. We have put several supplementary beams in place and thus it will last maybe two or three years more. Someday it will fall on our heads and that will be funny. Precarity enables us better to help the poor."[12]

2. What do you think of this perspective offered by the priest, held up by Dorothy Day?

3. How does precarity—think of it also as "unquiet" or "changeability"—as practiced in that monastery, relate to how people living secular lives might use and maintain the resources available to them?

4. What is the kingdom of heaven?

---

12. *Dorothy Day: Selected Writings*, ed. Robert Ellsberg (Maryknoll, NY: Orbis, 2005), 108.

Week One Prayer of Intention / Spiritual Practice

Make a list.

Make a list of ten things in your possession that you
have had for ten years or longer. Focus on the first ten
things that come to mind. Annotate each item with a
one-phrase or one-sentence description, remembering
when, where, or why you obtained it.

Scrutinize your list.

What draws you to each of these things you own? They
are probably harmless, simple, wonderful, and ordinary
things—why do you hold onto them? What makes each
one special?

Now, make another list.

List ten more things in your possession that you have
had for ten years or longer, which each mean less to you
than the ten things in your first list.

Ask yourself some questions.

Should I hold onto these things?

How would my life change if I lost one? Or all of
them?

Week Two

The Problem with Money

This week we are concerned not with possessions, but money. In the currency of current usage and practice, let's think of "money" as our ability to purchase what we need or desire. In Francis's day this meant purchase power for acquiring stores of supplies, and the ability to build buildings, institutions, and schools; these are the ways that religious orders and monasteries with vows of poverty are still able to have vast holdings of value. Also, of course then, as now, money meant coins in the pocket.

Francis made it clear that he despised coins and cash. The cash economy was just beginning when his apostolate began. His father was, in fact, a part of this fresh development in European commerce.

Many Franciscans who outlived Francis took with utmost seriousness Francis's disapproval of money. Long after Franciscan ministers-general and popes changed the austerity rules regarding poverty that had governed Francis's *Rule* during his lifetime, these followers, called *Fraticelli* or "the Spirituals," argued that when leaders and institutions of the Catholic Church don't live by absolute poverty they invalidate their authority to represent the founder of that Church, Jesus Christ.

One of these Spirituals, Angelo Clareno (ca. 1248-1337) imagined a gospel written by Jesus himself, describing the manner of his life and the meaning of his teachings, in direct relationship to the advent of Francis of Assisi. This text has Jesus reflecting:

> I preached penitence and the kingdom of the heavens wearing one tunic and a cheap cloak, opening the way of life to my disciples, walking as one with them without money, shoes, purse or wallet. Lacking a shelter, I, who made the heavens, had no place where I could lay my head, so that I might show to my imitators that the world and all the things that are of the world are to be considered and spurned like worn-out things and like dung.[13]

Angelo was trying to see Jesus in Francis's image, to argue for the absolute poverty of Francis's life and teachings. We can probably all agree that Angelo went too far.

The fighting within the Franciscan orders continued around these issues, and in 1317, when, with his bull *Sancta Romana Ecclesia* Pope John XXII abolished all dissident Franciscan groups, Angelo and others like him were forced to leave their friaries and affiliate with religious elsewhere.

Money causes problems of many kinds.

13.　Angelo Clareno, *A Chronicle or History of the Seven Tribulations of the Order of Brothers Minor*, trans. David Burr and E. Randolph Daniel (Bonaventure, NY: Franciscan Institute Publications, 2005), 3.

Reading 1

In Week One, we looked at accounts of the first friars who joined Francis in his way of life. Selling their possessions was of utmost priority. Here, we turn to Francis's own words, in the first formulation of the Franciscan *Rule*, to see how Francis thought money was an important consideration too.

The Earlier Rule
(The Rule Without a Papal Seal)
(1209/10-1221)

Chapter 2: The Reception and the Clothing of the Brothers[14]

If anyone, wishing by divine inspiration to accept this life, comes to our brothers, let him be received by them with kindness. If he is determined to accept our life, let the brothers be very careful not to become involved in his temporal affairs but present him to their minister as quickly as possible. On his part, let the minister receive him with kindness, encourage him and diligently explain the tenor of our life to him.

When this has been done, let the above-mentioned person—if he wishes and is capable of doing so spiritually without any difficulty—sell all his belongings and be conscientious in giving everything to the poor. Let

---

14.   *Early Documents: Vol. 1 (The Saint)*, 64-5.

the brothers and the minister of the brothers be careful not to interfere in any way in his temporal affairs, nor to accept money either by themselves or through an intermediary. Nevertheless, if the brothers are in need, they can accept, like other poor people, whatever is needed for the body excepting money.

When he has returned, the minister may give him the clothes of probation for a year, that is, two tunics without a hood, a cord, trousers, and a small cape reaching to the cord.

Reflect or Discuss

1. I remember wondering, when first reading of Francis's enthusiasm for Mt 19:21, why they sold their possessions, instead of just giving them away. What do you think?

2. What is the potential trouble with selling the possessions instead of giving them away: the acquiring of money.

3. What's wrong with money?

4. Look at some of the biblical passages that inspired Francis in these matters, for example: "Look at the birds of the air; they neither sow nor reap nor gather into barns, and yet your heavenly Father feeds them. Are you not of more value than they? And can any of you by worrying add a single hour to your span of life? And why do you worry about clothing?

Consider the lilies of the field, how they grow; they neither toil nor spin, yet I tell you, even Solomon in all his glory was not clothed like one of these" (Mt 6:26-29). How do his actions reflect his way of reading scripture?

5. The most common argument for bypassing these teachings is the responsibility one has for others. For example, a Franciscan in 1230 might have said, *If we don't buy books, how will we educate all the young men who want to become friars?* And a Franciscan in our day might say, *If I don't set aside money for my children to go to college someday, then they may not be able to go to college.* What do you think of these reasonings?

Reading 2

We read yesterday from the earliest version of Francis's *Rule* for life. In that same document, this then appears several chapters later. The warnings against money—whether it's coin in the hand or the ability to purchase something tomorrow—continue to be serious and uncompromising.

The Earlier Rule
(The Rule Without a Papal Seal)
(1209/10-1221)

Chapter 8: Let the Brothers Not Receive Money[15]

The Lord teaches in the Gospel: Watch, beware of all malice and greed. Guard yourselves against the anxieties of this world and the cares of this life.

Let none of the brothers, therefore, wherever he may be or go, carry, receive, or have received in any way coin or money, whether for clothing, books, or payment for some work—indeed, not for any reason, unless for an evident need of the sick brothers; because we should not think of coin or money having any greater usefulness than stones. The devil wants to blind those who desire or consider it better than stones. May we who have left all things, then, be careful of not losing the kingdom of heaven for so little.

---

15. *Early Documents: Vol. 1 (The Saint)*, 69-70.

If we find coins anywhere, let us pay no more attention to them than to the dust we trample underfoot, for vanity of vanities and all is vanity. If by chance, which God forbid, it happens that some brother is collecting or holding coin or money, unless it is only for the aforesaid needs of the sick, let all the brothers consider him a deceptive brother, an apostate, a thief, a robber, and as the one who held the money bag, unless he has sincerely repented.

Let the brothers in no way receive, arrange to receive, seek, or arrange to seek money for leper colonies or coins for any house or place; and let them not accompany anyone begging money or coins for such places. However, the brothers can perform for those places other services not contrary to our life with the blessing of God. Nevertheless, the brothers can beg alms for a manifest need of the lepers. But let them beware of money. Similarly, let all the brothers be careful of going throughout the world for filthy gain.

Reflect or Discuss

1. What does Francis say *before* saying none of the brothers should have money unless it is to care for the sick?

2. So, avoiding money is a guard against malice, greed, and too much care for the things of this world. Do you consider that a reasonable sort of guard? How was it reasonable then? How is it less reasonable now?

3. Francis seems to regard money itself as filthy, but then, at the end of this section, he also makes reference to the "pursuit" of money as "filthy gain." What is your response on either score?

4. We all almost certainly have to revalue these teachings for our lives today. How might you do that in your life?

Reading 3

There's an interesting story from the early life of Francis —as his conversion was in its early stages—of him following Jesus's instructions regarding poverty and then suddenly feeling self-conscious about the coins in his pocket.

The Life of Saint Francis
Thomas of Celano

Chapter 4: How After He Sold All His Belongings, He Despised the Money He Received[16]

Ah! Inclined and strengthened by the Holy Spirit the blessed servant of the Most High, seeing that the appointed time was at hand, followed that blessed impulse of his soul. Thus, as he trampled upon worldly things, he made his way to the greatest good. He could no longer delay, for by then a fatal disease had spread everywhere and infected the limbs of so many that, were the doctor to delay just a little, it would stifle breath and snatch life away.

After fortifying himself with the sign of the holy cross, he arose, and when his horse was made ready, he mounted it. Taking with him scarlet cloth to sell, he quickly came to a city called Foligno. There after selling everything he brought in his usual way, this successful merchant even left behind the horse he was riding, when

16. *Early Documents: Vol. 1 (The Saint)*, 188-90.

he had obtained his price. Starting back, he put down his bags and pondered conscientiously what to do about the money. In a wonderful way, in an instant, he turned completely to the work of God. Feeling the heavy weight of carrying that money even for an hour, and reckoning all its benefit to be like so much sand, he hurried to get rid of it. Returning toward the city of Assisi, he came across a church on the side of the road. It had been built in ancient times in honor of Saint Damian and was threatening to collapse because of age.

Arriving at this church, the new soldier of Christ, aroused by piety at such a great need, entered it with awe and reverence. He found a poor priest there, kissed his holy hands with great devotion, offered him the money he was carrying and explained his purpose in great detail.

The priest was astounded and, surprised at this sudden conversion in incredible circumstances, he refused to believe what he was hearing. Because he thought he was being mocked, he refused to keep the money offered to him. It seemed to him that Francis, just the day before, was living outrageously among his relatives and acquaintances and exalting his stupidity above others. But Francis stubbornly persisted and endeavored to create confidence in his words. He pleaded, begging the priest with all his heart to allow him to stay with him for the sake of the Lord. Finally the priest agreed to let him stay, but out of fear of Francis's parents did not accept the money. The true scorner of wealth threw it onto a window opening, since he cared for it as much as he cared for dust. For he desired to possess wisdom, which is better than gold, and to acquire understanding, which is more precious than silver.

Reflect or Discuss

1. What an interesting story this is. Uncomfortable with those fancy silks, Francis sells them; then he's suddenly uncomfortable with what he obtained in return for them.

2. What does he do, next? Why?

3. Do you think Francis had to do what he did?

4. In the last sentence, wisdom is described as "better than gold," and understanding to be "more precious than silver." Such a juxtaposition might seem strange. However, read and reflect on Proverbs 2:1-6:

My child, if you accept my words
  and treasure up my commandments within you,
making your ear attentive to wisdom
  and inclining your heart to understanding;
if you indeed cry out for insight,
  and raise your voice for understanding;
if you seek it like silver,
  and search for it as for hidden treasures—
then you will understand the fear of the Lord
  and find the knowledge of God.
For the Lord gives wisdom;
  from his mouth come knowledge and understanding.

Reading 4

Let's turn to two more short portions from Francis's *Earlier Rule*, as we seek to understand more about his concern regarding money and its effects. This is his money-consciousness turning to a way of living freely and creatively, without cumbrances.

The Earlier Rule
(The Rule Without a Papal Seal)
(1209/10-1221)

Chapter 14: How the Brothers Should Go Through the World

When the brothers go through the world, let them take nothing for the journey, neither knapsack, nor purse, nor bread, nor money, nor walking stick. Whatever house they enter, let them first say: Peace to this house. They may eat and drink what is placed before them for as long as they stay in that house. Let them not resist anyone evil, but whoever strikes them on one cheek, let them offer him the other as well. Whoever takes their cloak, let them not withhold their tunic. Let them give to all who ask of them and whoever takes what is theirs, let them not seek to take it back.

Chapter 15: The Brothers May Not Ride Horses[17]

I command all my brothers, both cleric and lay, that when they go through the world or dwell in places they in no way keep any animal either with them, in the care of another, or in any other way. Let it not be lawful for them to ride horseback unless they are compelled by sickness or a great need.

Reflect or Discuss

1. In your own words, sum up how the brothers should go through the world.

2. The first selection here—chapter 14—is a pastiche of quotes from the Gospels. You should look at them in context: Lk 9:3, Mt 10:10, Lk 10:5-7, and Lk 6:29-30.

3. For twenty-first century readers, what might be the equivalent of not keeping an animal, and not riding a horse?

4. What is creative about these teachings?

5. How would these teachings leave you free? What might "freedom" mean for a Franciscan follower of Jesus?

---

17. *Early Documents: Vol. 1 (The Saint)*, 73.

Reading 5

We step away here from the accounts of Francis's biography to look at the theological and spiritual reasoning and defense for the Franciscan poverty initiative, written a century and a half after Francis took those first few steps. The author is Bartholomew of Pisa and he writes this as part of an enormous work called *The Conformity*, in which he parallels the life and practice of Francis with that of Jesus.

The Conformity of the Life of Blessed Francis
to the Life of the Lord Jesus
Bartholomew of Pisa

Book Two
From *Jesus the poor and humble – Francis*
is united with poverty[18]

We are urged to embrace poverty by its power and its miraculous salutariness. Its power is evident, because it makes the man who possesses it:

First, clean. For he who does not love temporal things, keeps himself unstained by this world, as the Gloss on Jas 1:27: "Clean religion" etc. says.

---

18. *Early Documents, Vol. 4, Book Two (The Conformity)*, 148-49.

Second, close to God. The shepherds came to God from nearby, but the royal Magi came from afar, Mt. 2:1 ff.; Lk. 2:8 ff.

Third, free from burdens. Gregory says: He who takes from me a load of riches, frees me to run more swiftly.

Fourth, joyful. For poverty is a joyful thing: if it is not joyful, as Seneca says, it is not poverty.

Fifth, peaceful. For what in this life is more toilsome than to burn with earthly desires? What more peaceful, asks Gregory, than to strive after nothing of this world?

Sixth, tranquil. For, as Gregory says, the complete absence of worldly desire brings great tranquility of heart; and Seneca, as quoted above, says: On the road beset by brigands the poor man is at peace.

Seventh, free, because it frees him from the sin of seeking after riches, which makes man a servant of sin, as Scripture proclaims.

Eighth, acceptable to God. The poor were allowed by Nebuchadnezzar to remain on the land, while the rich were taken away from it, Jer. 52:15 f.

Ninth, pure and true, because poverty is a refining fire. It can also be concluded that the power of poverty is shown by the fact that it causes man to be adorned and enriched by all the virtues. For the vale of covetousness has many pits of pitch, that is, of sins, but poverty has none, and leads us to heaven. This is shown by the poor Lazarus, who was carried into Abraham's bosom by the angels, while the rich man was buried in hell, Lk. 16:19 ff.

Reflect or Discuss

1. This passage asks us to reflect on the benefits of poverty. What are the first few that are mentioned?

2. Remembering your reflections from yesterday's reading, how does this prompt you to consider—or re-consider—the questions of creativity and freedom?

3. How is "poverty a refining fire"?

4. How might this refining fire relate to what Jesus said in Mt 5:3: "Blessed are the poor in spirit, for theirs is the kingdom of heaven."

5. If sincere followers of Christ have never been poor a day in their lives, what does that mean for their salvation?

Reading 6

To finish this Week, let us look at Francis at his most severe in his teaching about money—coins and currency.

The Beginning or Founding of the Order
John of Perugia

From *Chapter 6: The Brothers' Manner of Living and the Love They Had for One Another*[19]

One day while the brothers were staying at Saint Mary of the Portiuncula, some people came for a visit. They entered the church and placed some money on the altar without their knowledge. Then, one of the brothers, entering the church, took the coins he had found, and put them on the church's windowsill. Another brother, when he found the money where the other one left it, took it to Saint Francis.

When blessed Francis heard this, he diligently asked which one of the brothers had placed the money there. When he found out who it was, he ordered him to come to him. "Why did you do this?" he said. "Didn't you know that I want the brothers not only to avoid using money, but also not even to touch it?" When the brother heard this, he bowed his head, confessed his fault on his knees, and asked that a penance be given him. Francis

---

19.   *Early Documents: Vol. 2 (The Founder)*, 47-48.

then ordered him to carry the money out of the church in his mouth and, when he came upon some ass's dung, to place the money upon it. The brother very diligently fulfilled this. Then Francis admonished the brothers that whenever they found money, they should scorn it and consider it worthless.

They were constantly rejoicing, for they had nothing that could disturb them. The more they were separated from the world, the more were they united to God. These men entered upon a narrow and rough trail. They broke up the rocks, trampled upon the thorns, and so have left us, their followers, a smooth path.

Reflect or Discuss

1. The people who placed money on the altar were doing what they thought was appropriate—giving to the work of the church. What was wrong with that?

2. Francis's attitudes and responses to money were clearly radical, then and now. We also know that his religious order grew faster than any order ever had, up until that point. What does this suggest?

3. In Francis's day, money (in coins) was of less certain value than it is today, when the value of money is usually reliable and relatively constant. How does this perhaps explain why Francis so easily and ardently taught his friars to scorn the coins they saw as worthless?

4. Today, as then, money can unite us with the world and its concerns in ways that then subtly separate us from God. How does that happen?

Week Two Prayer of Intention / Spiritual Practice

If you live in a large city where you meet homeless people on the streets, or people begging on street corners regularly, you'll have easy opportunity for this practice. If you don't live in such a place, then do this the next time you go to a city. Or—even—go to the city simply to practice this.

Go to the bank and get a roll of quarters for ten dollars; or better yet, get a stack of dollar bills. Put the money in your pockets.

Each time someone asks you for a handout, don't even think about it: reach into your pocket and take a few quarters, or a dollar bill, and hand it to them.

Look them in the eye. You needn't say anything except for, "Here you go." If they say, "Thank you" or "God bless you," then respond with "You're very welcome" or "God bless you."

Don't pause to consider their worthiness to receive what you have. This is not to say that there are good reasons not to give to everyone in every circumstance—but see what it feels like, and then afterwards reflect on what it meant to you not to think, but simply to respond with a "yes."

Reimagining a Vow of Poverty

We have spent two weeks exploring what poverty meant to Saint Francis, and how it was central to the energy and spirit of the earliest Franciscans. Now, let's turn to reimagining poverty for our lives today.

Are we supposed to imitate Francis by selling everything we own, and by never carrying money, or having money to spend? Very few followers of Jesus, or Franciscans of any stripe, would answer "yes" unequivocally to those questions. We tend to equivocate on these matters today, and that isn't necessarily wrong.

Modern life is complicated. Religious life is complicated. Choosing how to walk the Franciscan way requires appropriating the truth of Saint Francis in a faithful, twenty-first century milieu. This week, we'll begin to try to do that.

Reading 1

There is being poor, and then there is living in the spirit of charity. These are not necessarily the same thing.

This extraordinary passage from Thomas of Celano's first biography of Francis recounts some of Francis's spiritual practices relating to poverty and his teachings on a life of charity. It leads us to ponder for ourselves how to reimagine a vow of poverty in the twenty-first century.

The Life of Saint Francis
Thomas of Celano

Chapter 28: The Spirit of Charity and the Feeling of Compassion for the Poor that Glowed in Him and What He Did with the Sheep and the Lambs[20]

The father of the poor,
the poor Francis,
conforming himself to the poor in all things,
was distressed to see anyone poorer than himself,
not out of any desire for empty glory,
but from a feeling of simple compassion.
Though he was content with a ragged and rough tunic,
he often wished to divide it with some poor person.

---

20.   *Early Documents: Vol. 1 (The Saint)*, 247-48.

This richest poor man, moved by a great feeling of pity, in order to help the poor in some way, used to approach the rich people of this world during the coldest times of the year, asking them to loan him their cloaks or furs. As they responded even more gladly than the blessed father asked, he used to say to them, "I shall accept this from you only on the condition that you never expect to have it returned." The first poor man who happened to meet him, he would then clothe with whatever he had received, exulting and rejoicing.

He was deeply troubled whenever he saw one of the poor insulted or heard a curse hurled at any creature. It happened that a certain brother insulted a poor man begging alms, saying: "Are you sure that you are not really rich and just pretending to be poor?" When Saint Francis, the father of the poor, heard this, he was deeply hurt and he severely rebuked the brother who had said these things. Then he ordered the brother to strip naked in front of the poor man and to kiss his feet, to beg his forgiveness. He used to say: "Anyone who curses the poor insults Christ whose noble banner the poor carry, since Christ made himself poor for us in this world." That is also why, when he met poor people burdened with wood or other heavy loads, he would offer his own weak shoulders to help them.

Reflect or Discuss

1. Empathy seems to be behind Francis's emotion and responses in the situations recounted here. Living in poverty, voluntarily or involuntarily, does

Week Three

not necessarily make you empathetic. What *does* make someone empathetic?

2. "The coat unused in your closet, belongs to the poor," said St. Basil the Great in the fourth century (and Dorothy Day, in slightly different language, in the twentieth century). Francis, who read very little, would have known this quote and this teaching. But how does he takes it a step further?

3. Consider the insult paid to the poor man by one of the brothers. What circumstances in your own experience does this accusation remind you of?

4. What is the overall message of how a follower of Christ, or Francis, is to treat the poor?

5. On the other hand, is the overall message about how to treat the poor . . . or about something else?

60

Reading 2

Here, we go deeper into the nuances of Francis's teaching, and begin to discover the spiritual nakedness implied in a Franciscan vow of poverty. This excerpt, taken from a text called the "Mirror of Perfection" or *A Mirror of the Perfection*, focuses more narrowly than other biographical sources on Francis's relationship to being poor in Christ.

*A Mirror of the Perfection, Rule, Profession, Life
and True Calling of a Lesser Brother*

From *Chapter 13*[21]

Often when blessed Francis was honored and people said, "This man is a saint," he would respond to such expressions by saying: "I am still not sure, since I might have sons and daughters." And he would say: "If at any moment the Lord wanted to take back the treasure He has loaned to me, what would I have left except just body and soul, which even non-believers have? I must believe, rather, that if the Lord had granted a thief and even a non-believer as many gifts as He has given me, they would be more faithful to the Lord than I."

He continued: "As in a painting of the Lord and the Blessed Virgin on wood, it is God and the Blessed Virgin who are honored; God and the Blessed Virgin are held

---

21. *Early Documents: Vol. 3 (The Prophet)*, 224.

in memory. The wood and the paint attribute nothing to themselves because they are merely wood and paint. In the same way, a servant of God is a painting, that is, a creature of God, in whom God is honored because of His goodness. Like wood or paint, he must not attribute anything to himself, but give all honor and glory to God. He should not attribute anything to himself while he is alive except shame and trouble, because, while he is alive, the flesh is always opposed to God's gifts."

Reflect or Discuss

1. What does Francis mean by saying, "since I might have sons and daughters"?

2. What do you make of it that he leaves room for the possibility that he might turn unfaithful to his vows?

3. Do you remember our look at "precarity" in Reading 6 of Week One? How does this anecdote refer to precarity in Francis's life (and in our lives)?

4. Perhaps you've heard the teaching of Jesus about being perfect. It goes like this: "Be perfect, therefore, as your heavenly Father is perfect" (Mt 5:48). Reflect on this. Then consider the verse immediately before it, also said by Jesus: "[I]f you greet only your brothers and sisters, what more are you doing than others? Do not even the Gentiles do the same?" (Mt 5:47)

5. We usually think of "perfect" as meaning "flawless"; but it also can mean "mature."How does our understanding change if we substitute the word "mature" in Mt 5:48 for the word "perfect"?

Reading 3

Let's now look at the first of two excerpts from a text called *The Anonymous of Perugia*, or *The Beginning or Founding of the Order*, another of the earliest biographical narratives about Francis and the early friars. We see in more detail how goods in common were handled between the friars and in their friaries, and how this might relate to our reimagining a vow of poverty in our day.

The Beginning or Founding of the Order
John of Perugia

From *Chapter 6:*
The Brothers' Manner of Living and the Love They Had for One Another[22]

Whatever they had, a book or a tunic, was used in common and no one called anything his own, just as it was done in the primitive church of the Apostles.

Although extreme poverty abounded in them, they were always generous, and spontaneously shared the alms given them with all who asked for the love of God.

When they went along and came upon poor people begging from them, some of the brothers would give them some of their clothing, since they had nothing else to give. One of them even tore the capuche from his

---

22.   *Early Documents: Vol. 2 (The Founder)*, 46-47.

tunic and gave it to a poor beggar; while another tore off a sleeve and gave it away; and still others gave away a part of their tunic to observe that Gospel passage: Give to all who ask of you.

One day a poor man came to the church of Saint Mary of the Portiuncula where the brothers were staying and asked for alms. There was a cloak there that one of them had while he was still in the world. Blessed Francis told the brother, whose cloak it was, to give it to the poor man. He freely and quickly gave it to him. And immediately, because of the reverence and dedication that the brother had in donating the gift, it seemed to him that the alms rose up to heaven and he felt himself filled with a new spirit.

When the rich of this world went out of their way to visit them, they received them quickly and kindly, and would invite them to call them back from evil, and prompt them to do penance.

At that time, the brothers would eagerly beg not to be sent to where they had been raised so that, in this way, they would avoid association and dealings with their relatives and observe the words of the Prophet: I have become an outcast to my brothers, a stranger to my mother's sons.

They rejoiced most in their poverty, for they desired no riches except those of eternity. They never possessed gold or silver, and, although they despised all wealth of this world, it was money especially that they trampled under foot.

Reflect or Discuss

1. Consider this quote from Dorothy Day, from April 1964: "The mystery of the poor is this: That they are Jesus, and what you do for them you do for Him. It is the only way we have of knowing and believing in our love. The mystery of poverty is that by sharing in it, making ourselves poor in giving to others, we increase our knowledge of and belief in love."[23]

2. How might Francis's commitment to poverty be connected to Day's understanding of being poor in order to learn about love?

3. What is the kingdom of heaven?

4. When the author quotes the one he calls "the Prophet," it is in fact a psalmist: "I have become an outcast to my brothers, a stranger to my mother's sons" (Ps 69:9). Francis and many early friars were comforted in their faith as distinct from what they found at home and among their biological families. How does this strike you? Does it influence your view of faith and family?

5. Notice the common use of items between the friars. What do you think keeps us from sharing more things in common with our neighbors and friends today?

---

23. *Dorothy Day*, ed. Ellsberg; 330.

Reading 4

This short, intriguing anecdote reveals more aspects of Francis's character and personality related to his views and way of life regarding the practice of poverty. Similar episodes appear in many of the biographical sources we have.

The Remembrance of the Desire of a Soul
Thomas of Celano

The Second Book
Chapter 42: The Saint Is an Example in Seeking Alms[24]

So that he might never offend his holy bride even a single time, this servant of the Most High God would do as follows: whenever he was invited by some lord and was to be honored by a more lavish dinner, he would first beg some pieces of bread at the neighboring houses, and then, enriched by poverty he would hurry to the table. Sometimes people asked why he did this, and his answer was that he would not give up a permanent inheritance for a fief granted for an hour. "Poverty," he said, "not your false riches, makes us heirs and kings of the kingdom of Heaven."

---

24. *Early Documents, Vol. 2 (The Founder)*, 295-96.

Reflect or Discuss

1. Who is the "holy bride" of Francis mentioned in the opening line?

2. The Wisdom of Solomon in the Apocrypha, for example, uses a feminine image of the Divine to remind the Israelites who led them out of bondage in Egypt and through the wilderness: "She [Sophia] gave to holy people the reward of their labors; she guided them along a marvelous way, and became a shelter to them by day, and a starry flame through the night" (Wis 10:17).

3. Consider how a passage from Matthew's Gospel (15:35-37) may have inspired Francis in his practice of poverty as narrated here. "Then ordering the crowd to sit down on the ground, he took the seven loaves and the fish; and after giving thanks he broke them and gave them to the disciples, and the disciples gave them to the crowds. And all of them ate and were filled; and they took up the broken pieces left over, seven baskets full."

4. Reflect on Jesus's parable in Mt 13:24-30 and how it relates to Celano's anecdote: "The kingdom of heaven may be compared to someone who sowed good seed in his field; but while everybody was asleep, an enemy came and sowed weeds among the wheat, and then went away. So when the plants came up and bore grain, then the weeds appeared as well. And the slaves of the householder came

and said to him, 'Master, did you not sow good seed in your field? Where, then, did these weeds come from?' He answered, 'An enemy has done this.' The slaves said to him, 'Then do you want us to go and gather them?' But he replied, 'No; for in gathering the weeds you would uproot the wheat along with them. Let both of them grow together until the harvest; and at harvest time I will tell the reapers, Collect the weeds first and bind them in bundles to be burned, but gather the wheat into my barn.'"

5. Francis refused lavishness. In your own commitment to poverty, what might you refuse today?

Reading 5

A ponderous and challenging text, this one, and it will
continue in tomorrow's reading. It is taken from a source
known in early Franciscan history as a mystical classic.
Ubertino da Casale, one of the most important leaders
in the half-century after Francis's death, wrote this on
Mount LaVerna, the Mount Sinai of Franciscanism. He
said that his work was inspired by the Holy Spirit.

Ubertino describes the pedagogy of the man who
fell in love with holy Poverty, but still, as we all do, had
to discern how to live with her. We all need the inspiration of the Holy Spirit to do this.

The Tree of the Crucified Life of Jesus
Ubertino da Casale

From *Book Five, Chapter 3*
The Virtue of Poverty[25]

We have already said that virginity, humility, and
poverty were the outstanding signs of Christ Jesus and
of His coming, and the first two have been somewhat
examined. The third, poverty, has been constituted the
hidden treasure by Jesus, Wisdom of the Father, for the
acquiring of which everything must be sold. He himself
led others by His example to observe it and decreed that

---

25.   *Early Documents: Vol. 3 (The Prophet)*, 159-60.

evangelical perfection consists in poverty. For on this rock upon which the evangelical house is founded, no floods dashing into it can swamp it, no winds or downpours can shift it, no gales can knock it down. To this virtue Jesus has consigned the undisturbed possession in this life of the kingdom of heaven; whereas to the others He has merely promised its future possession. Because those who imitate true poverty in fervor of spirit must, of necessity, live off celestial fare. Because they give no thought to earthly wares and relish instead, during their present exile, the delicious crumbs that fall from the table of the angels, this is that most exalted virtue of Christ Jesus on which His unique seal is imprinted on those who strive to observe it throughout the course of their perfection. For the one who shall espouse this virtue with fullness of faith, most fervent love and unsullied observance will be lacking in no perfection. Not only is this poverty a virtue; it is the perfection and queen of all virtues. For she lays the very summits of all the virtues under her surveillance and above all, those who yield to her wishes she shapes to the likeness of Jesus, Son of God, by a renewal in which the perfecting of every state consists.

Accordingly Francis, emulator of the likeness of Jesus from the outset of his conversion, applied his every effort to seek out holy Poverty and to follow her totally, ever eager to observe the likeness of Christ. He hesitated before no adversity, feared no menace, shrank from no toil, sought to avoid no physical discomfort, if only he could enjoy the embraces of Lady Poverty.

Reflect or Discuss

1. Poverty is referred to as "the hidden treasure," which is a reference to Mt. 13:44: "The kingdom of heaven is like treasure hidden in a field, which someone found and hid; then in his joy he goes and sells all that he has and buys that field."

2. Consider how odd it is that poverty is described as something to be purchased. What might that mean?

3. How might a reimagined poverty, less stringent than Francis's vow, somehow still be the "perfection . . . of all virtues"?

4. How might voluntary poverty and detachment be related? Let's look at an example from outside religious life. Arlo Guthrie writes about his father, Woody Guthrie (folk singer-songwriter, author of "This Land Is Your Land"): "When I was very young, I remember an evening when my father chose to sleep on the floor instead of a bed. I asked him why. He told me he didn't want to get soft. He wanted to remain detached from comfort so he could come and go without distraction. From his friends and peers, I heard stories of him getting a new car, or guitar, or something of value, only to give it away when it ran out of gas or needed new strings. He had very clearly learned the first lesson of what we identify in spiritual life as detachment. The same was true in his relationships (much to the chagrin of family relatives, and co-workers). He had

learned from a very young age that attachment to things, people, or places would only lead to the burden of sorrow. . . . He learned he could enjoy almost anything without needing to possess everything." (*Woody Guthrie: Songs and Art, Words and Wisdom*, by Nora Guthrie and Robert Santelli. San Francisco: Chronicle Books, 2021; 303.) What similarities do you see between Woody Guthrie's spirituality of detachment, and Francis's life of poverty?

Reading 6

This last reading of Week Three is a continuance from Reading 5, as in an imagined one-way conversation with Jesus Francis comes to understand the truth.

The Tree of the Crucified Life of Jesus
Ubertino da Casale

From *Book Five, Chapter 3*[26]
The Virtue of Poverty

This inquisitive explorer began his search in the streets and in the squares of the Church, questioning individuals from different states of life on how they loved Gospel poverty. The expression he used seemed obscure, almost uncouth to his listeners. None of them ever heard of it, recoiled from the very mention of it, and practically reviled him for questioning them. "May the poverty you seek always be with you, your children and your seed after you." They said, "We should be allowed to enjoy the good things of life in affluence."

When Francis heard this from those of a common state, he said, "I'll go to the supreme pontiffs, and speak with them. Surely they have long known the way of the Lord and the judgment of God. These commoners perhaps are unknowing and foolish, ignorant of the paths

---

26. *Early Documents: Vol. 3 (The Prophet)*, 160-62.

their own Lord Jesus trod." Yet those pontiffs responded more harshly. "What," they said, "is this new teaching we are hearing? Who could exist without temporal possessions? Are you better than our ancestors who gave us temporalities and occupied well-endowed churches? What is this poverty that tells us little? We do not know what you are talking about."

Francis was amazed. Drunk with the spirit of poverty, he turned to the pursuit of prayer and began to invoke Jesus, the teacher of poverty:

"O Lord Jesus show me the pathways of your beloved Poverty. . . . For I . . . languish with love for her nor can I find rest without her. My Lord, you know it, you who loved me because of her. But even she sits in sorrow, rejected by all. . . . She, queen of all virtues, is now moaning on her dunghill because her friends have all betrayed her and become her enemies, and these are the very ones who for long have proved themselves adulterers and not spouses.

"Look, Lord Jesus, how poverty is the great queen of the virtues, for the reason that You, leaving the angelic dwelling-places, came down to earth that You could espouse her in perpetual charity and in her, from her, and by her produce all the sons of perfection. And she clung to You with such fidelity that Your esteem for her began in Your own mother's womb, for You had, as is believed, the most diminutive of human bodies which, once it came forth from the womb, found its rest in the holy manger and stable. As long as You lived in the world, You so deprived yourself of everything as to lack even a place to lay Your head. . . . And though the disciples abandoned You and denied Your name, she did not forsake You. . . .

"At that time Your own mother was alone in devoting herself to You and languishing with love for You as she joined in Your sufferings. Yet even for such a mother the cross was too high to reach and touch you. But Lady Poverty, destitute of everything, like Your dearest handmaid was embracing You more closely than ever before, her whole heart involved in Your torments. . . . [W]hen You were dying of burning thirst, that faithful spouse was there to assist You. For when You could not obtain a little water, she made up a drink from what she could get from shameful lackeys, which was so bitter that You could only taste it rather than actually drink it. And so in the close embrace of Your spouse You breathed Your last.

"Oh, who is there who would not love this Lady Poverty above all other things? I beg You that I be signed with the entitlement that is hers to give. I desire to be enriched with the treasure she is. O most poor Jesus, I petition You, for the sake of Your name, that this be the property my brothers and I will have for ever, namely, never to be able to own anything under heaven. And let this flesh of mine, as long as it lives, be sustained always, though in utter frugality, by fare that comes from others."

The Kindest One granted his petition by putting into his heart and revealing to his mind an understanding of poverty's height and gave him the desire to imitate it to the full.

Reflect or Discuss

1. Note how unique and personal Francis's questioning was, and how the leaders of the Church did not know the answers.

2. Note the personification, again, of Poverty, and how she was there like Mary at the Crucifixion.

3. If you knew Lady Poverty in the way that Francis seems to have known her, would poverty be easier to accept, and to live?

4. How much is our understanding of the Christian life, in all respects, dependent upon our meeting God—as Father/Mother, Christ, Holy Spirit—and knowing God intimately?

Week Three Prayer of Intention / Spiritual Practice

Compose a prayer or a poem, or if you prefer, simply a paragraph of your desire, to Holy Poverty. With the divine personification of Poverty in mind, what would you say to her now, to express your own desire to know her, find her, and live with her in a new and meaningful way?

The Sacred Exchange between Saint Francis and Lady Poverty suggests, for example, that Francis used phrases from the third chapter of the Song of Songs to express his own pursuit:

> Upon my bed at night I sought him
> whom my soul loves;
>
> I sought him, but found him not;
>
> I called him, but he gave no answer.
>
> "I will rise now and go about the city,
> in the streets and in the squares;
>
> I will seek him whom my soul loves."
>
> I sought him, but found him not.
>
> The sentinels found me,
> as they went about in the city.
>
> "Have you seen him whom my soul loves?"
> (Sg. 3:1-3)

Week Four

Living Poor for Others

So why is the Kingdom of Heaven first and foremost for the poor? This seems unfair, doesn't it? What is it about being poor that naturally entitles one to favor with God? Is it a sort of karmic reward—since things were bad for you here, they will be better for you in the next life? No.

New Testament theologians explain it differently, and helpfully. Their answer is basically this: Only the poor and the destitute, the lonely and the suffering, fully recognize their ultimate inability to act to save themselves.[27] They cannot do so. They know that they can't. To them, first and foremost, comes the faith in God that saves. This is why Francis was so insistent on being poor in every sense of the word—not simply through personal poverty, but corporate poverty, meaning that he could not rely on structures and safety nets, as the truly poor cannot either.

In our day, Pope Francis has focused a great deal on mission and evangelization as central to a Christian life, and he doesn't mean by those words saving people's souls. He means loving people fully and effectively, as followers of Christ are required to do, but often do so poorly.

---

27.   See for instance Joachin Jeremias, *New Testament Theology*, trans. John Bowden (New York: Scribner's, 1971), 117-19.

In remarks on the tenth chapter of the Gospel of Luke, Pope Francis said:

> To offer one's life in mission is possible only if we are able to leave ourselves behind. . . .
>
> At the root of every Christian vocation we find this basic movement, which is part of the experience of faith. Belief means transcending ourselves, leaving behind our comfort and the inflexibility of our ego so that we can center our life in Jesus Christ. It means loving, like Abraham, our native place and going forward with trust, knowing that God will show us the way to a new land. This "going forward" is not to be viewed as a sign of contempt for one's life, one's feelings, or one's own humanity. . . .
>
> All of this is profoundly rooted in love. The Christian vocation is first and foremost a call to love, a love which attracts us and draws us out of ourselves, "decentering" us.[28]

In this final Week, we will focus on how a commitment to poverty enables our commitments to mission and to loving. We will turn from what not to do—or, what not to own, possess, and protect—in order that we might do other things.

---

28. Pope Francis, *The Gospel of Luke: A Spiritual and Pastoral Reading* (Maryknoll, NY: Orbis Books, 2021), 119-120.

Reading 1

As we've said a few times already, Francis did not view himself or his ministry as unique so much as a continuation of the Gospel life of Christ and Christ's disciples, in any era.

This first reading, taken from the same source by Ubertino da Casale that we were introduced to last week, emphasizes this. It mentions some of the events of Francis's life which have appeared in earlier readings and weeks in this book, as well.

The Tree of the Crucified Life of Jesus
Ubertino da Casale

From *Book Five, Chapter 5: Jesus Established the Form*[29]

Jesus, the perfection of our whole created world, established in His own life, and in that of His Mother most amiable, the gospel life in all its fullness, as though upon the holy mountains and on unshakable foundation. While the virgin born of that virgin with her most holy motherhood in extreme poverty, in the most profound humility He was humbled, obedient to the law and to His eternal Father, even to the hard offering of the cross in a perfect act of virtue and an enduring contemplation of the divine. In an inseparable bond they lived, loving

---

29.   *Early Documents: Vol. 3 (The Prophet)*, 195-96.

their enemies, laying down and offering their entire life in death for the salvation of their enemies alone. For He had no friend except the one whom He met out of love for His enemy.

Hence the *Rule* of gospel living is founded in Christ Jesus and in His most holy mother and, by analogy, Christ passed this on, His own perfection, to the Apostles with the command that they observe it. For these reasons, it is not alone an evangelical *Rule*, having been established in and by Christ, but also an apostolic *Rule*, for it was laid down for the Apostles by Christ Jesus, and they kept it till their deaths. It was not passed on by them to the Church, however, as we have pointed out already, and it was unknown in the Church when the blessed Jesus began to renew it in Francis. That this was so can be clearly seen in what the *Legend*'s Third Chapter tells us of Francis's petitioning the lord Pope to confirm his gospel life. To some of the cardinals it seemed novel, something arduous and beyond human powers. Which, of course, is nonsense; this would be to revile the Gospel of Jesus Christ. It is, therefore, obvious that Jesus made Francis the foundation of the evangelic and apostolic *Rule* in the Church, as far as its restoration was concerned.

That this might be what He imposed more widely is clear from the first motive, from the development in between, and from the conformity to the end, and by an observing deed and by explaining his intention.

For his motive was listening to the Gospel of the sending out of the apostles; when it was said that they were sent to preach, He gave the disciples an evangelical way of living, that is that they should not have gold or silver, a wallet or purse, or two tunics, walking stick, or shoes. For, with the unending fervor of his heart, Francis placed all his eagerness into fulfilling all that he had heard, and he transformed his uprightness into an apostolic rule. And, in the Gospel, Christ did not impose on the apostles anything except what he said to everyone, that they should take up the cross. Therefore Francis formed his habit according to the teaching of the Crucified in the form of a cross, that a crucified mind might fight under a crucified tunic.

Reflect or Discuss

1. "Jesus made Francis the foundation. . ." it says here. "He gave the disciples an evangelical way of living." There is a sense here that Francis simply had to pick it up and carry it.

2. Ubertino refers to suggestions that Francis's way of life seems arduous or "nonsense." How do you see his life?

3. Look at the last paragraph and reflect on the idea of having a "crucified mind." What does that mean?

4. One discipline taught to many Third Order Franciscans is making a last will and testament. How might willing our possessions to others, after our death, connect with living a vow of poverty?

Reading 2

This reading also comes from the half-century after Francis's death. We continue to see how early Franciscans understood the saint's life, this time from Saint Bonaventure.

Here, Francis the founder of religious orders and a reformer of the gospel way of life, is portrayed as suffering for others.

From *The Morning Sermon on Saint Francis, 1267*
Bonaventure of Bagnoregio[30]

First of all, Saint Francis is commended . . . by the mouth of God for his deep humility: Behold my servant whom I uphold. What the Lord says in Haggai may be applied to him: In that day I will take you, O Zerubbabel my servant, and make you like a seal, for I have chosen you. This text says: I will make you like a seal and that by the signs and marks of the passion impressed on you by the Word of the Almighty. And why does he say this? Because Saint Francis was a servant of God, humble in his reverence for Him, more humble still in caring for his neighbor, and most humble of all in despising himself. I admire the humility of Saint Francis more than all his other virtues.

---

30.   *Early Documents: Vol. 2 (The Founder)*, 749.

He was a humble servant of God in the reverence he had toward Him. For this reason what the Lord says in the Book of Job may be applied to Saint Francis: Have you considered my servant Job, that there is none like him on the earth, a blameless and upright man, who fears God and turns away from evil?

God calls Job his servant on account of his humility. He was committed to God's service and reckoned a servant of outstanding reverence for God because he was blameless in his motives, upright in what he chose, God-fearing in his feelings, and turned away from evil in his actions. In all that he did and suffered he praised God. Moreover, we read of Job that there were born to him seven sons and three daughters. The name Job is interpreted "sorrowing," and this truly describes Saint Francis, because his life was filled with sorrow.

Reflect or Discuss

1. Bonaventure holds up Francis's humility, more than another other quality or virtue. How might we embody humility in our lives today?

2. Consider humility in light of climate change and the necessity of eliminating fossil fuels. This will lead to a different lifestyle for us—a humbler lifestyle, to be sure.

3. Pope Francis writes about this in *Laudato Si'*, for example: "Sobriety and humility were not favorably regarded in the last century. And yet, when there is a

general breakdown in the exercise of a certain virtue in personal and social life, it ends up causing a number of imbalances, including environmental ones.... Once we lose our humility, and become enthralled with the possibility of limitless mastery over everything, we inevitably end up harming society and the environment." (#224)

4. How may our lives become more Franciscan in very ordinary ways, such as planting gardens and fixing things rather than throwing them away?

5. Might flying on airplanes become, in the present and future environmental crisis, similar to what riding on horses once was, to Francis?

Reading 3

A few paragraphs later, Bonaventure's sermon from 1267 adds the following.

From *The Morning Sermon on Saint Francis, 1267* *Bonaventure of Bagnoregio*[31]

Second, this servant of God was humbler still in caring for his neighbor. As Saint Paul writes to the Corinthians: For though I am free from all men, I have made myself a slave to all. Our holy Father Francis became all things to all men and the servant of everybody. He wanted even to be the servant of the most despised. And once, walking along the road, he promised obedience to one of his brothers. When he was still in the world he had a great loathing for lepers. But after his conversion he devoted himself to taking care of them. He washed their feet, bandaged their ulcers and sores, cleaned away the pus and rotten blood, and kissed their feet. He cared for his neighbor to this extent in order to make himself contemptible and to implore God's grace. Saint Paul tells the Galatians: For you were called to freedom, brethren; only do not use your freedom as an opportunity for the flesh, but through love be servants of one another. Such should our freedom be.

---

31.   *Early Documents: Vol. 2 (The Founder)*, 750-51, 753.

Someone might object that while it is true we must serve our neighbor, we are not obliged to serve lepers. But God himself did not disdain this kind of service. He bent down to wash the dirty feet of his disciples, and then said to them: "You call me Teacher and Lord; and you are right, for so I am. If I then, your Lord and Teacher, have washed your feet, you also ought to wash one another's feet. For I have given you an example, that you also should do as I have done to you."

. . . If someone owned a precious gem which the more worthless it was considered, the more precious it became, how willingly he would show it to those who disparage it. Strength of spirit increases through reproaches; what folly it is, therefore, to seek praise. The Saints wanted to be despised by others in order to be pleasing to God. As Saint Gregory says: "If holy people who achieve so much, reckon themselves as practically worthless, what is to be said of those puffed up with pride, yet devoid of virtue?" Saint Anselm tells us that there are six degrees of humility, and he who succeeds in arriving at the sixth, possesses the fulness of grace. The first degree of humility is to account oneself despicable; the second is to speak of oneself as despicable; the third, to convince others that one is despicable; the fourth, to want to be judged despicable; the fifth, to want to be spoken of as despicable; and the sixth, to want to be treated as despicable. At this point one is close to God and is his humble servant.

Reflect or Discuss

1. Look at 1 Cor 9:19, which he quotes at the start: "For though I am free with respect to all, I have made myself a slave to all, so that I might win more of them."

2. To what, and for what, might Francis want to "win" them?

3. Notice the gem mentioned in the final paragraph, different from the treasure mentioned in Reading 5 in Week Three; this gem is, in fact, worthless, and it is its worthlessness that makes it precious. What does this mean?

4. Francis sought to discover his despicability. There's really no sugar-coating this—that's the word, and there really are no synonyms for "despicable" that will make it sound more palatable to our twenty-first century ears. How can we reimagine ourselves as despicable for God, today?

Reading 4

A life of poverty is not just about not owning, not possessing, and not protecting things, but by concerning our lives with other things in place of those usual concerns. So today's reading looks at Francis's essential teaching of being like a mother to others, encouraging us to look closely at how the qualities of motherhood are perhaps what Francis had in mind for every person wanting to walk the Franciscan path.

The Beginning or Founding of the Order
John of Perugia

Chapter 6:
The Brothers' Manner of Living and the Love They Had for
One Another[32]

Each time they saw one another, the brothers were filled with such delight and spiritual joy that they forgot all the adversity and the extreme poverty they had suffered.

Every day they were conscientious about prayer and working with their hands to avoid all idleness, the enemy of the soul. At night, they were equally conscientious about rising in the middle of the night according to that passage of the Prophet: At midnight I rise to give you thanks and they prayed devoutly with frequent tears.

---

32.   *Early Documents, Vol. 2 (The Founder)*, 45-46.

They loved one another from the heart and each one served and took care of the other, as a mother serves and cares for her son. The fire of love burned so intensely in them, that they would have willingly sacrificed their lives not only for the name of our Lord Jesus Christ, but also for one another.

One day, two brothers were walking along a road when suddenly a simpleton began throwing stones at them. One of them, seeing that a stone was about to strike his brother, ran directly in front of him. Because of ardent mutual love, he preferred that the stone strike him rather than his brother. They frequently did these and similar things.

They were rooted and founded in love and humility, and one would respect the other as if he were his master. Whoever among them excelled because of a position or gifts of grace, seemed even more humble and self-effacing than the others.

Reflect or Discuss

1. This text was probably written fourteen years after Francis's death, in the fall or winter of 1240-41, by a friar who knew the early followers of Francis well. He heard and repeated stories that they told. Notice how it begins with reference to their poverty. Where does it then go?

2. Busy hands that avoid idleness. Rising in the middle of the night. Loving one another with great

care. How does motherhood encompass all these qualities and activities?

3. How might poverty make spiritual motherhood possible?

4. How might spiritual motherhood be impossible without some measure of poverty?

5. How are intentional poverty and spiritual motherhood both countercultural?

Reading 5

We move from motherhood to fatherhood and other ways of living for others.

A Book of the Praises of Saint Francis
Bernard of Besse

From *Chapter 3:*
The Self-Emptying of Blessed Francis[33]

At times he endured a very great temptation of the flesh and, to put this temptation to flight, he would scourge himself unmercifully. But when this spirit would not depart despite the severe discipline, he would cast himself naked into the snow. It was by this chastisement of his flesh that he expelled the spiritual wound from his breast.

At another time a very serious temptation of spirit came upon him. . . . [H]e was filled with anguish and sorrow; he afflicted and chastised his body, he prayed and wept bitterly. He was under attack in this way for several years, until one day while praying at Saint Mary of the Portiuncula, he heard in spirit a voice: "Francis, if you had faith like a mustard seed, you would tell the mountain to move from here, and it would move." The saint replied: "Lord, what is the mountain that I could

---

33. *Early Documents, Vol. 3 (The Prophet)*, 43-44.

move?" And again he heard: "The mountain is your temptation." And he said, sobbing: "Lord, be it done to me as you have said!" At once, after the whole temptation was driven away, he was set free.

His spirit emptied itself with humility, cherishing everyone, deferring to everyone. He used to revere priests of the Church; would respect the elderly, and honored the noble and the wealthy. He loved the poor intimately, however, and, while preserving peace with people of all rank, he urged his brothers eagerly to this. He used to tell them: "As you announce peace with your mouth, may you keep it in your heart, thus no one will be provoked to anger or scandal, but rather to kindness and gentleness. For we have been called to this: to cure the wounded, to bind up the broken, and to recall the erring. Many who seem to us to be members of the devil, will yet be disciples of Christ."

To his brothers he would speak compassionately, not as a judge, but as a father to his children and a doctor to the sick, so that the word of the Apostle might be fulfilled in him: Who is weak that I am not weaker? Great was his compassion toward the sick and great his concern for their needs. He conducted himself toward all as he would toward individuals. As he scrutinized with dignified honor any revered person coming to the Order and respectfully gave to each his due, he wisely considered in all matters the dignity of rank of each one. He was truly endowed with outstanding discernment and the grace of simplicity, so that with a true dove-like simplicity, he possessed the prudence of a serpent.

Reflect or Discuss

1. Francis's temptations don't seem to have to do with riches or property; but how are some of us tempted by these things?

2. What might it mean for us to be "set free" from the temptations of security, which we might say is the opposite of being voluntarily poor?

3. Weakness and compassion are virtues extolled toward the end of this reading. How are weakness and compassion enabled by poverty?

4. He is called a father who is weak, dove-like, and simple. Does that sound like a father to you? Would those be good qualities in a father?

5. How is self-emptying an aspect of your reimagined vow of poverty?

Reading 6

We are concluding with this portion from *The Conformity* in part because of a phrase in the middle of it, referring to Francis's "joyful and genuine love of humble and rejected persons." Vulnerability—this is the extension of poverty to consider in this final reading.

The Conformity of the Life of Blessed Francis to the Life of the Lord Jesus
Bartolomew of Pisa

Book Two
From *Francis abases himself*[34]

Humility, the guardian and ornament of all virtues, so completely governed our Father, the man of God blessed Francis, that, although he shone with the privilege of manifold virtues, it was this virtue that seemed to have attained a special sovereignty in him, being as he was the least of the Lesser. Indeed it was upon this virtue that he laid the foundation of his holiness, he observed it in the actions of his life, and at length at his death it went with him in glory to be crowned in heaven. If we are therefore briefly to consider his humility, as we did that of Christ in the first part of the above exposition of

---

34. *Early Documents, Vol. 4, Book Two (The Conformity)*, 208-9.

the Fifth Conformity, there are many remarkable facts
that bear witness to the humility of blessed Francis.

The first is his joyful and genuine love of humble
and rejected persons. This love of blessed Francis for
humble people is shown by his affection for the poor. . . .
For since he was liberal and generous, as much by nature
as by a gift of grace, he gladly gave them alms.

. . . [H]e stripped himself of his own clothing and
gave it to a poor knight. When he was in the world he
would pile his table with loaves so that he could give to
the poor. And he bound himself to the Lord with a vow
that, whenever he possibly could, he would deny nothing to those who begged "for the love of God," and he
kept this vow until his death, giving everything he had
at his disposal to the poor. He demonstrated this in the
beginning by his association with the poor and humble.
When he was in the world, he dressed in their clothing
and took his place among the poor outside the door of
the Church of Saint Peter to beg alms with them. In
the same place, that is, at Rome, when he was invited to
supper by Matteo Rubeo, he lowered himself onto the
ground with the poor folk who had been invited to eat by
that lord, and ate with them.

His love for despised and humbled persons, specifi-
cally lepers, is spoken of in the *Legend of Three Companions*
and the *Major Legend* Part I. For before he renounced the
world, while he was praying blessed Francis heard from
the Lord that he must love what he hated and that what
formerly he found sweet would be bitter, and at length
he must find sweetness in those things at which he had

formerly shuddered; and then Christ appeared to him fastened to the cross, and said to him: "If you will be perfect and come after me, deny yourself and take up your cross and follow me," and afterwards blessed Francis had a special love for lepers. Once when he was out riding, as we read in the *Major Legend* Part I, he came across a leper, and although he was overcome with revulsion, he got down from the horse and gave him money and a kiss. He then mounted the horse again and when he looked behind him the leper was nowhere to be seen.

Reflect or Discuss

> 1. Again, the virtue of virtues in Francis's life is humility, but this time, the emphasis of humility's activity in his life is to serve the humble, the rejected, and the despised.

> 2. How does a life of poverty make this possible?

> 3. How would a life of wealth, comfort, and security make this impossible?

> 4. What is a poor person but vulnerable? Francis's poverty was voluntary, and as this text makes clear, so was his vulnerability. But it was also God-directed.

> 5. How is your poverty, your vulnerability, being directed by God?

Week Four Prayer of Intention / Spiritual Practice

Where will your poverty and vulnerability take you? We cannot be poor and vulnerable all alone by ourselves. If you've made it this far in this book, I think it is safe to assume the Holy Spirit is speaking to you. Be sure that you're listening for what comes next.

So spend time in prayer today, and again tomorrow, and then the next day. Take little time speaking. Listen instead.

You may want to conclude your sitting sessions with these familiar words, which were not composed by Francis of Assisi, but echo his spirit most beautifully:

> Lord, make me an instrument of thy peace.
> Where there is hatred,
> let me sow love;
> where there is injury, pardon;
> where there is doubt, faith;
> where there is despair, hope;
> where there is darkness, light;
> where there is sadness, joy;
> and all for thy mercy's sake.
> Divine Master,
> grant that I may not so much seek to be consoled
> as to console;
> to be understood as to understand;
> to be loved as to love;
> for it is in giving that we receive;
> it is in pardoning that we are pardoned;
> and it is in dying that we are born to eternal life.

FOCOLARE MEDIA

Enkindling the Spirit of Unity

The New City Press book you are holding in your hands is one of the many resources produced by Focolare Media, which is a ministry of the Focolare Movement in North America. The Focolare is a worldwide community of people who feel called to bring about the realization of Jesus' prayer: "That all may be one" (see John 17:21).

Focolare Media wants to be your primary resource for connecting with people, ideas, and practices that build unity. Our mission is to provide content that empowers people to grow spiritually, improve relationships, engage in dialogue, and foster collaboration within the Church and throughout sociecy.

 Visit www.focolaremedia.com to learn more about all of New City Press's books, our award-winning magazine *Living City*, videos, podcasts, events and free resources.

NEW CITY PRESS